Whatever Happens to BABY HORSES?

By Bill Hall

Illustrated by Virginia Parsons

MERRIGOLD PRESS • NEW YORK

© 1965 Merrigold Press, Racine, Wisconsin 53402. All rights reserved. Printed in the U.S.A.
No part of this book may be reproduced or copied in any form without written permission
from the publisher. All trademarks are the property of Merrigold Press.
ISBN: 0-307-90962-X   MCMXCI

Baby horses! They run and jump like puppies and kittens, and they want to be friends with everyone. They nibble on clover and they nuzzle their mothers. Their coats are fuzzy. Their tails are short and their legs are long. Whatever happens to baby horses?

The first thing that happens is that the baby horse, or foal, wants to stand up as soon as he is born. But this is hard for him to do. His legs are all mixed up.

Very soon, he does stand up. Then he tries to walk. His legs are nearly as long as his mother's legs, but they are not very strong yet. Plop! He falls down.

The baby horse tries again. He gets his legs straightened out and starts to walk. He wobbles over to his mother to get some of her milk. The milk makes him strong enough to wobble around some more. Then he takes his first nap.

When he wakes up, the baby horse has some more milk. Now he can walk much better. Soon he can trot.

Then he can GALLOP. Around and around he goes in circles. But when he gallops too fast he falls down. He gets right up and starts all over again.

The baby horse's neck is so short and his legs are so long. In the pasture, he has to bend his legs to reach the grass. Or he finds some grass that he can reach without bending over. He has four teeth. His mother is proud of him. She fans him with her long tail.

The baby horse's coat is brushed by his kind owner
who will teach him many things before he is a grown-up
horse.

What does the baby horse learn? First he learns how to run fast without falling. Then he gets used to wearing his halter so that he can be led about by his owner.

Soon he has learned to eat from his own feed box.
And he has a stall of his own. Sometimes his mother
looks over the wall to see if he is happy.

He can't be called a baby horse, or a foal, any longer.
He is a colt now. He is learning how to pull a cart.

When he is about two, this colt learns to carry a rider. And then he is taught how to jump over fences, for that is what he will be—a jumper. He will win prizes and make his owner proud. No one would guess that this fine, big horse was once a baby horse with a fuzzy coat and a short tail.

That is what happened to one baby horse. But whatever happened to this baby horse?

He is in the rodeo.

And whatever happened to this baby horse?

He works on a farm.

And whatever happened to this baby horse? She was gray when she was born.

She grew up to be white!
Now she is in the circus.

Big horses, little horses, fast horses and slow horses, all kinds of horses work hard for people who treat them well. When they go out into the fields to graze, sniffing the green grass—walking, running or just standing still—do you suppose they are thinking of when they were baby horses?

Like this one? For you.